The First Day

Beth Gordon

BELLE POINT PRESS

Fort Smith, Arkansas

THE FIRST DAY

Cover image: Pay Phone, Getty Images Signature
via Canva Pro License

Edited by Casie Dodd
Design & typography by Belle Point Press

Belle Point Press, LLC
Fort Smith, Arkansas
bellepointpress.com
editor@bellepointpress.com

Find Belle Point Press
on Facebook, Substack,
and Instagram (@bellepointpress)

Printed in the United States of America

28 27 26 25 24 1 2 3 4 5

ISBN: 978-1-960215-27-7

CHAP16/BPP36

Contents

The remember isn't a road

Marianne Boruch

The First Day (2010)

We woke up the next day & the remember was sitting on the floor just inside the bedroom door. This was the first of many surprises. That shampoo was needed was the second. I do want to remember your skin. The smell of your neck like a field of tobacco. Before is a circle of trees. The inner bark peeled to reveal pale white wood. As white as my thighs. I'm sure there were mulberries. I don't mean mulberries & you inside the bedroom door. I mean I want the mulberries to always be. Before is a crow walking across the black asphalt parking lot. Before is a crow with one eye on the eastward floating cloud. Clouds without decipherable shapes. Now they are flying dogs or blooming sunflowers. The crow. The clouds. The mulberries. The empty shampoo bottle. No shampoo & a funeral waiting. I do remember what the text said. I don't remember if you were telling the truth. Never is the pair of amber earrings. Never is the pay phone inside the laundromat. Never did I have enough quarters. We woke up the next day after the next day & you were not washing your hair. Never is a shower or a shopping list. The bedroom door is always open. We are gliding in or out.

Sunday

THIS MORNING MY mother told me a new story. She said I've told you this before, *right?* Her mother's people, the Heaths. They made their living in marketing. I don't think they called it that she said. She's probably right. Although the word was coined in 1897. Her mother's people—the Heaths—were long entrenched in the Piedmont. Where the dirt sticks to your soles like tar. She said they hired a group of wiry boys who passed out flyers in downtown: advertisements for the drugstore, the grocer, the butcher, the movie theater, all three funeral homes. She said, my grandpa Heath was excommunicated from the Methodist church for square dancing. *I always loved that about him.* Look, I get it: you're tired of my obsession with death. Me too. But this story of the boys, the flyers, the movie theaters with their black & white diamond earrings & cocktail glasses: the man who called out *swing your partner.* Every story my mother tells me is full of ghosts. I'm getting to the point, I promise. Kerry Ann called last night. Kerry Ann with her father who died one month before Daisy. Kerry Ann who danced with me in bars from west of the Missouri to just north of Springfield, IL. Kerry Ann who I called when my orange cat died in 10 seconds of a heart attack: she came right away with a shovel & a bag & never told me where she buried him. Kerry Ann who drove me to Florida in a car that would not shift to reverse & failed to mention that detail until I was 1,000 miles from home. *I think I'm calling to say goodbye* she said just last night. She's dying, cancer dancing through her body from pancreas to liver. She's dying & I'll be the last of the three: Neecie, Kerry Ann & me. I always knew I'd outlive Kerry Ann: she's been chasing death for years. Chasing death in run-down cars & horses too wild to ride. But how could I have guessed that one bitter February morning just last year Neecie would lift a bag of groceries, unlock her garage door & fall to the floor. A stroke as big as a dragon. No one there to call the ambulance. Not for hours. Neecie with her red hair & Scottish brogue that thickened when she was angry. Neecie who made me laugh a week after my granddaughter died. Neecie who cussed with such flair. Do you remember 1995? I know now that the woman in Charlottesville in the Russian gift shop was an amber-scented ghost. Future ghost like that Christmas story. But nothing like that at all. I know now that we were also ghosts. Ghosts of the present day. But the present day keeps moving. Who can keep up? It was 1995 or 2022. The world is ending all the time. We are so aware of our certain demise: every generation is sure it is the last. Look, maybe we are the last generation: but what if this really *is* a simulation? What if *The Matrix* is a documentary? What if the marketers & pharmaceutical companies are god's messengers & much maligned? I'm with you: my obsession with death is boring & predictable. The days are closing in & November is waiting like a noose. It's

Sunday morning again & my mother stands in her garage as I drive away. I'm always surprised at how tiny she is. I'm always surprised that there is a story I haven't heard. She was next to me on the sofa when Kerry Ann called. She said *you have to answer*. She knows my face & voice so well: she took my hand while I asked what the doctors had said. She squeezed my hand while Kerry Ann went down one of her broken-transmission-but-let's-drive-to-Florida-and-hope-for-the-best rabbit holes. Something about leaning backwards over a well. Something about rolling a cigarette before she called. Something about her sisters who won't talk to her anymore. Who can keep up? What she means is be safe. What she means is why didn't you love me enough to stay. Listen, I know you're asking the same question. I know you've read this far to find the answer. But I have to tell you about my Russian maintenance man. Boris. How he used to scoff at my broken garbage disposal: my broken bathtub faucet. My need for the dishwasher to run without noise. *What'd you do* he asked: meaning how can you be this careless? *Why you take baths* he asked: meaning aren't there enough people drowning beneath the ice? I know now that he had a point. I know now that he was the ghost of the past. He laughed at the ways we worry about the apocalypse. What did we think? Of course it's all going to end. Transmissions & shovels & drains.

The First Day (1995)

THE ROAD WAS as perfect as a prairie dog at dawn. Empty sky. Nose-kissed. Eyes forward & open in the morning wind. The surgeon general warned us often. Tobacco on your tongue tasted too good. Too good to consider dead ends. As good as caramel ice cream melting on my skin. God knows. We were too young to die. You told me to ignore the oracle. Ignore the tarot card. I should not have listened. I should have stared down the barrel of the crystal ball. Watched the road drop off. Never did I leave the whirling laundromat. Should have let you lose the backseat game. Could have spared us both. Like hydrangeas in mid-September. We said one more hour. One more hour in the light. Strawberry moon. Come save us from the ditch. Never should have let you take my glasses off.

Saturday

My daughter is driving through hurricane wreckage. She calls me to tell me she's safe. She says the pier is gone. *Remember,* she says, the tattooed man with the parrots? He knelt down to share bright feathers with Theodore. Theodore who refused to enter the ocean. Theodore who played in the wet & silky sand. Later: we took him to the ice cream shop. *It's all gon*e she says. But I already know. I've seen the pictures online. The videos of rubble & ruin. The drone footage. Which is one thing I can discuss in a before & after kind of way. My life before drones. My grandchildren's lives after. Where machines record hurricanes eating the highway. She called me just yesterday to say they never lost power. I'm trying so hard not to think about death today. But you see where I'm going with this. Don't you? Less than a week ago Kerry Ann called. Now she says she's not dying after all. The power of prayer. Prayer & ketamine. Her doctor was amazed. Turns out so am I. Bridges are collapsing all around us, but she remembers. She remembers everything. The time she was four years old & living in Montana & her father left her with strangers for two weeks. I'm not supposed to write about death anymore, but the news keeps shouting through my phone. Nobody left me with strangers. My babysitter a closet hippie who taught me how to draw caterpillars & frogs, how to fringe the edges of my only pair of blue jeans. How to train my fingers with number 2 pencils to hold the perfect formation to flip someone off. I'm not making this up: I can raise my middle finger with a kind of balletic grace thanks to Marty the babysitter. Marty, short for Martha, a name she said she hated. We baked sugar cookies & took them to the lake where her boyfriend rubbed baby oil onto her freckled shoulders. A muddy Midwest lake with unidentifiable shadows beneath our legs. I don't know why I didn't drown: why the boyfriend didn't drive the car into a tree while Marty stroked his thigh: why the house didn't burn down when we left the oven on 325 degrees for over four hours. My daughter says the grocery stores are only taking cash. The line of cars at the gas stations looks like a scene from *Mad Max*. Kerry Ann is calling again & I know I won't answer. I cannot listen to the X-rays of her wreckage. Listen, I know that this is not the point in the story where I mention my mother's cousin, Dinah. Dinah who said, *I'm never going back*. Dinah who jumped off the tallest building in downtown. I know this is not the point in the story where I tell you that the trees outside my window are glistening like starfish tossed onto the broken shore. This is not the point in the story to mention that there are bodies that will never be found. If I'm honest, I'll confess I rarely write sober: I'm certain it's a failure of my imagination. I killed a spider just last night: another failure of imagination. Or compassion. I'm still trying to decide if the difference is worth noting. I killed a spider just last night & this morning my car wouldn't start. Do you see where I'm going with this? How can I keep track of time: how can I understand the second hand's circular penetration: how can I tell you what day it is when the storms are tossing ice cream shops into the abyss? The eyewall of the hurricane hovered over my daughter's home for over four hours. My daughter brought the chickens inside. Listened to the wind howl like a train without a track. Let the kids open every container of playdough. Knowing that Magnolia would rather press her face against the tenuous glass. Knowing that Theodore would combine every color: roll them into a ball until the pink & purple, orange & green, red & purple, all melted into a grayish planet of despair. Yes, I've done it again. Yes, endings are on my mind. So is the young man who arrived to jump the battery in my car. As wiry as boys with newspapers: shouting the headlines for a penny or piece of bread. He said, *sorry it took me so long.* He said he stopped to change a flat along the way. I cannot forget his mountain accent: a mixture of pine needles & sand. My mother still believes in the power of prayer. Although she says that Grandpa Heath never went back to church. He did keep square dancing, though. She tells me about her Great Uncle Cecil. How he came home once a year & was never around when the babies were born. How everyone knew about his girlfriend. How he bought her nylons & groceries in full view of the town. How he was just another weak & drowning man. She says, *I never knew him well.* Listen, I know now you are wondering where to find the ghosts. Let me point the way. Cousin Dinah. The tattooed man who cradled parrots in his arm. Marty's brother left to drown in the torrential rains of Vietnam. Every starfish who was burrowing in the shallow end before the storm. Kerry Ann, a ghost in the graveyard of her life: also her father. The spider in my closet. I pulled into my mother's garage this morning with my freshly charged battery. With a grocery bag full of ice cream. With a tenuous belief that new stories are through the door. I'm supposed to stop talking about the ways our days will collide. I'm supposed to turn the key without fear of explosion.

The First Day (2000)

FIRST, I MUST say something (kind) about the father of my children (his eyes were blue like Santa Claus). First, I must say something (I remember) about the father of my children (he laughed at my white cotton bra). My children want me to say something (true) about their father (he burned down every room with his smile). On the road to Charlottesville you said things. Your mouth sparked like a lighter. The smell of Camel cigarettes: the bloom of your tongue. First, I must confess that I sinned. Against God (the father). The father of my children not on this road trip. Against the Holy Ghost (he covered my face with a pillow). The father of my children not on this road (on our way to an ice cream shop). (He left me alone in every hospital). First, I must remember strawberry cream.

Friday

JD DREAMED I won a skateboarding contest. I receive this information by text. He & my mother cheered me on as I twisted through the streets like a sparrow. Hugged me between them when I crossed the finish line. He says he didn't sleep well last night. The crowds. The hum of fiberglass wheels. His certainty I would fall & crack my skull. My mother left to arrange another funeral. Or pay for the breathing machine. I never signed the DNR: never bothered to draft a will. Construct a list of my assets & debts. I dreamed I was in the yellow house with my ex. Not a skateboard in sight. There was so much to say but instead I was listening to the faraway drone of whale song. There was so much to say but instead I was listening to the clack of billiards. The clink of quarters in the jukebox. The sound of my father's feet on the pier. Another text arrives with details of the trophy. Details of the smell of fried catfish hovering over the race. Also today is my birthday. Also the last skateboard I rode was wooden with chipped sky-blue paint: chipped ceramic wheels: a wooden ramp at the bottom of the hill. Also I should not mention death on the anniversary of my birth. But who am I to argue with our dreams? One year on my birthday I walked down the aisle. Aflame in purple: bolstered by Valium. Moved into the yellow house. The yellow house where Annabelle sledded down the stairs on flattened cardboard boxes. The yellow house where Annabelle dared her sisters & stepsisters & neighborhood boys to jump off the roof with a sheet as a parachute. One year on my birthday I did not understand that 8 days later Annabelle would die in a car. I received this news by text. I was in my red Chevrolet on a Friday afternoon. *L.A. Woman* on the radio. Stopped at the railroad tracks: a slow train in no hurry. I was in no hurry to drive home. Walk into the red brick house & tell my children that Annabelle had flown away from us like a twilight of blackbirds. One year on my birthday I was in a hospital bed. Cradling my first-born child like an unopened parachute. I'm not supposed to question the power of prayer, but it turns out my suspension of disbelief was left on the highway. Sweltering like roadkill at mile marker six hundred & two. Turns out there's not enough chocolate cake in this world to suppress my useless rage. Turns out Boris the maintenance man was right about my bathtub drain. One year on my birthday I danced in JD's kitchen. A diptych painting of a train cradling my shadow. A bottle of tequila in my hand. In all the photos of that night I am looking up. In all the photos of my granddaughter she is looking up. If I'm not talking about her death: who am I? If I'm not watching mass-shooting documentaries. If I'm not shepherding my mother through grief's winding streets. If I'm not counting the number of loved ones who disappeared without warning in the last 12 years. If I'm not counting backwards to Wednesday. If I'm not walking through the hospital hallway towards the blue, fluorescent light. Who am I? One year on my birthday my parents forgot to celebrate. After the hall light turned off, I crept down the stairs & drank half a bottle of their sherry. I saw them on the dining room table. My mother says this never happened. She says it must have been a dream. But I remember the sweet & bitter liquid on my tongue. I remember that my father never told her when I came home past my curfew. One summer morning in Nebraska in 1972 I rode my skateboard down the hill while the neighborhood boys were still sleeping. I still wear the scars on my chin. My stomach. My left knee. My most sacred scars. I have so many things to say about 1972. My parents were as beautiful as Hollywood. As beautiful as grasshoppers. As beautiful as my wet knees in the bathtub. My mother was a feather bed. My father was in love. My mother was a glowing ember: stoked. I danced to the Partridge Family in our suburban driveway. I danced to Three Dog Night: Joy to the World. Road to Shambala. *One is the loneliest number*. I sat on the top step while my parents danced. As beautiful as patent leather shoes on Easter Sunday. I was as invisible as a light bulb. One year on my birthday my mother dropped my cake in the parking lot. One year on my birthday I asked for a 1 a.m. curfew. A pair of blue jeans. *Frampton Comes Alive* on 8-track tape. One year on my birthday: I was born.

The First Day (1987)

MAYBE IT WAS Amarillo. Bonnie in the room next door. Offering tepid beer. An invitation to mud wrestling. Or Idaho. A town too small to name. Jukebox & cowboys & Mormons with red manes. You went out for lunch. Maybe the sweaty alleyways. Mobile, AL. New Orleans. Santa Fe. But no. We left at dawn & drove the opposite way. You left the office to stand in line. To smoke beneath a tree. Cigarette against your tongue. You told the secretary to answer. Maybe it was Santa Barbara. Mountain to my left. Ocean to my right. No. I forgot you that night. Not a dial tone in sight. I whispered in nickel postcards. How do moonlit lovers know what to say? I got back in the tired car. What to do with all that loose change? They tore down the last pay phone in NYC just yesterday.

Thursday

THE BLACK CAT doesn't live here anymore. I'm sorry to say I was never able to decipher his words. The black cat had eyes as green as rhododendron leaves in June. As green as jelly beans in the cold April grass. As green as seaweed in the Mississippi Bay. My daughter announces that she is in love. Not the daughter who calls me from the eye of the hurricane. My other daughter who texts me pictures of her two gray cats. The one who leans into the camera: the one who howls for more food. The black cat ran under the sofa & refused to be bribed with soft tongues clucking against the roofs of our mouths. My upstairs neighbors built a cage on their small wooden deck. Left their dog in it for hours & days. Howling. Urinating. Frightened & alone. I am guilty of leaving many living creatures frightened & alone. I am guilty of refusing to open my home to spiders. Beetles. The old man who waves to me from across the parking lot. The green-eyed cat who bit my hand one too many times. I'm getting to the point I promise. My daughter who lives in a cobble-stoned city with her two gray cats. My daughter who sells plumbing supplies & holds her own in a world of foul-mouthed men. My daughter is in love & there's nothing but sunshine in her voice. *Dancing Queen* is on the radio & JD tells me a story I haven't heard. 2005 & multiple margaritas & multiple friends: some long dead. A lawyer, a dentist & a teacher walk into a bar. Karaoke on the menu. *Dancing Queen* on the screen & JD sang *feel the beat from your tambourine.* Sang all the high parts & 17 years later tells me how they borrowed sober friends to drive them home. How Connie wouldn't sleep on his sofa for fear of her husband's wrath. I didn't know him then: still 9 years away from a funeral party: a table full of crackers & cheese & julienned carrots: my lover in another room. My lover whose daughter died three years before. We argued the entire way. Argued about which exit to take. Argued about where to park the car. About how I was supposed to smile in a room full of mourners 4 short months after my granddaughter died. My daughter is in love & here I am again. Talking about funerals & ghosts: past/present/and future. My daughter is in love & all I can think about is the show *Lost.* All I can think of is how *Lost* premiered in 2004 long before I re-named each day. My daughter is in love & Thursday is my favorite day. A day without hangovers or predetermined parties. A day that lives under your skin like new car smell. A day that opens like a field of wheat. Also nobody I loved ever died on a Thursday. That I know of. But I promise I'm not looking. Not scouring obituaries to find a Thursday funeral. Happy to live in the pre-coffee haze of un-knowing. Do *you* remember that show *Lost*? It started with an eye. A dog. A fiery plane. A beautiful cast of castaways stuck in a time machine disguised as an island. Or maybe it was an island disguised as purgatory. Or purgatory disguised as a mixtape of all our mistakes. In

2004, Thursday was the day after every new episode of *Lost*. A day to stand at the receptionist's desk & discuss Charlie & the submarine. Or Hurley & the way he believed the VW bus with no engine would start. How it did start & the radio played *Road to Shambala*. Now Thursday has a new name: *After the Ambulance Before the Train*. Now it's KC & the Sunshine Band on the radio & JD says they were Connie's favorite. She would travel far & wide to see them. Never worried about exits or parking spaces. Never worried about planes splitting in two. Fire signals. Singing in tune. It's Thursday. The weather is alive. My gray-eyed daughter is in love.

The First Day (2013)

I MUST NOT think about the streetlights. I must not say the streetlights were shimmering like rain. We crossed the tracks ahead of the metro train. It wailed like a warning in the rear-view mirror. I must not think about the car lights ahead: left or right. The way the bridge rose into the sky as we crossed to the other side. I must not remember the vibration. My ragged cowboy boots. The phone lit up like a campfire. The streetlights. The ambulance light: red & circling like a crow. The train we left far behind. You lit a cigarette. You said it will all be fine. The parking lot signs that guided us. The door opened like the mouth of a tunnel. I must not think about lights. Your cigarette's glow. Bedroom lamp flickering in the thick of a storm. Garden solar lights pop on as the sunlight starts to whistle away. I must not think about the phone. The text you sent three years before. The shadow on the wall. The waking up tomorrow. The door snapped behind me as I stepped into the awful light.

Wednesday

I HAVE SO much to say about 1972. I have so much to say about polyester pants & polyester body suits. Multi-orange shag carpet. *The Godfather*. Every grownup whispering about a horse head & all that blood. Whispering between the benediction & final hymn. Whispering beneath the dentist assistant's hand. Whispering at the breakfast table. My brother & I crumbled bacon into our scrambled egg sandwiches. My mother with half a grapefruit. My father kissing her head. His hair was as shiny & black as his shoes. His gleaming eyes. I know that 1972 is not the point. Except I was safe. I was a safe & beloved child. Yes, there were whispers. The two boys who disappeared from the school Halloween parade. Later found butchered in an empty November cornfield. Yes, there was an angry German shepherd chained to a purple school bus on our daily walk home. Yes, I inserted my body between my brother's body & the bullies who saw the softness in his eyes. Yes, I punched a boy in the mouth & he bled & I will never forget the thrill of his tearful scream. Yes, I was just a girl, but my knees were always shredded. Bicycles, skateboards, dirt roads, 5th grade boys who didn't understand why my brother listened to Beethoven. Why he read encyclopedias. Why he could never connect the wooden bat to the leather ball. I'm not saying that I understood. I'm saying he could never beat me in checkers or kickball or standardized tests. But one day he led me into a bookstore & showed me all three volumes of *Lord of the Rings*. One day he took me to the movie theater to see *Yellow Submarine. Journey to the Far Side of the Sun. Young Frankenstein. Silent Running.* Later: *Jaws* & *Star Wars* & one day the 5th grade boys jumped him at the bus stop. I still have the ragged scar—raised & red from years of road tar lingering just below the skin. I'm not saying that I understood. I'm saying I was a safe & beloved child & the world is a dangerous place. I'm saying that in 1982 I was in a hotel bar in Wheeling, WV with my father. He asked for the wine list & they brought us a small leathery menu with red ribbon for flair. Boone's Farm Green Apple embossed on its pages with a 5-star review from the hotel's staff. It was 1982 & we laughed like teenagers watching *Animal House*. I'm saying in 1992 I lived in a beige townhouse in Leesburg, VA & heard Kurt Cobain on MTV. The walls were beige, the appliances were beige, the carpets were beige, my womb was failing to cooperate inside the colorless space. It was 1992 & Kurt's dirty hair was as beautiful as a starfish. I'm saying in 2002 I was a single mother of 3 ferocious children in a 2-bedroom apartment across the square from the old newspaper building. Below us without a thermostat of her own lived Bobbi who married a roughneck in 1952 & now refused to be coaxed into the storm cellar when the tornado sirens wailed. I'm saying in 2012 my daughter told me she was pregnant & I was angry & empty of benediction. I was ready to empty the nest. I was a red &

flaming scar & 6 months later I held the most beautiful child ever born. I'm saying that I tried to protect my brother but one year the snow in Japan was so deep that he & his wife had no food for a week. One year he flunked out of college & mowed lawns all summer before joining the military. One year he cried in my parents' garage because he did not know how to change the oil in his car. He did not understand the whispered secrets of violent men. Did not know how to stop the bleeding of a split lip. Look, you see by now, don't you? 1972 is not the point of any of this. Now it's 2022 & on my kitchen wall is a sketch of yarrow in a plastic frame that I bought for a dollar one week before my father died. I'm saying that I knew the truth about the world, but I looked away. I looked away & she was gone. On a Wednesday night. All the Halloween candy sorted in neat piles. The costumes: princess & werewolf, pumpkin & puppy, ballerina & monster: packed in an attic box. A week later the snow was whispery & fierce. She was not there to feel its sting. One year we pooled our money together. 18 quarters in hand. We bought *The Fellowship of the Ring. The Two Towers. The Return of the King.* 50 years later & my brother feeds the poor from his empty pockets. My mother gave away her car. The old scar on my knee glares back at me: red as a new burn. My pollen-dusted granddaughter 9 years gone. The tattered books live in my home. The only things I could ever save.

The First Day (undated)

THERE ARE DAYS that begin like this: I don't want to leave the bed: but the bed is a puddle of snakes: I don't want to leave the bed: but each snake has a color & flavor: if I wait here in my pajamas the snakes will tell me their names. I don't want to leave the bed: but the purple snake tastes like burnt hair. I don't want to leave the bed: but the red snake is named Delilah. The red snake brings me scissors. If I leave the bed the snakes will sink into the mattress: tiny clams at the ocean's edge: if I leave the bed the walls will stay walls: gray as birch trees: gray as summer rain: gray as winter asphalt in March when my father forgot his way. I don't want to leave the bed: pulling a blue snake from my hair: her blue eyes are a small glisten of drowning: there are these days. The kitchen is so far away: the hallway is a catastrophe of fun house mirrors: the kitchen is a lemon tree: the kitchen is a lemon cocktail: the kitchen is a lemon drop stuck in the back of my throat: the hallway is a minefield of maps & one-way signs: the quicksand floor is a flashing arrow: merge/right lane ends: the kitchen is waiting like a desert highway: but I don't want to leave the bed. Someone is brewing coffee & I know it isn't me: I'm still memorizing the blue snake's name: someone is brewing coffee in the kitchen & I know it isn't me: the blue snake is as blue as a broken heart on the last day of the year: if I follow the lemon seeds into the kitchen: I'll forget the blue snake's name: who is brewing coffee: there are days that begin like this. I don't want to leave the bed: but my ocean is singing in the kitchen. We donated the car yesterday: the silver car with a sultry face: the silver car that my father drove to the ocean: the silver car where I stared at my father's silhouette & knew the snakes had crawled into his brain: he had forgotten the language of maps: his clockwork brain a puddle of golden sycamore leaves. We donated the car yesterday & my mother said *her name is Grace.* This morning: I don't want to leave the bed: the blue snake's name is Grace: my father was a nest. My father was a mongoose. My father knew the way to everywhere: the words to disperse a chorus of snakes: to make up a bed with perfect hospital corners: down the hallway of possible flame: into the yellow kitchen: my father is brewing the coffee. There are days that begin without coffee or my father or the silver car: without our feet in sand: without jukeboxes or his brown eyes: I don't want to leave the bed. There are days in the middle of cornfields: stalks as tall as my beautiful father: cobwebs in the corner of the garage. We donated the car yesterday & couldn't find the wrench: his tools laid out in rows like sweet summer corn & tomatoes that open like mint. Sandpaper: drill bits: there are days in the middle of a hardware store: oil & pine & following him down every aisle to find a can of lemon paint: the bed is full of snakes: the back door is open: the baby wrens are awake.

Tuesday

It's three days after my birthday & I'm explaining my life to JD. Or if not my life, exactly, I'm trying to explain my job. Resumes & executive assessments & the way I am paid a living wage to judge my fellow humans. I'm a magic mirror of half-lies: a metal detector for all the things left unsaid. A cog in the corporate elevator. A repository for thousands of life stories reduced to what they can remember about their last three jobs. I'm not saying I'm proud of this. I'm saying there's a poison called money that I swallow every day. I'm saying that there are only two degrees of separation between my existence & every person who has let me wade in the dangerous waters of their past. It's three days after my birthday and we are talking about every job we've ever held. JD tells me that I don't know about the levels. He used to write test questions for the SAT organization. Another sanctioned method of judgment. He said the first level is basic recall. Implying that memory is the lowest form of functioning. Implying that everything I'm writing here is suspect. Memory is like an escape room. Which is a weird thing for me to say because I would never pay money to be trapped inside unfamiliar walls & asked to work with a team of my best friends to find the unlocked exit. I've always been bad at directions. When my youngest daughter was six years old, she led me from one end of Six Flags to the other because my contact lens had crawled up under my left eyelid & I needed to find a mirror. Even without this impediment I would have not been able to retrace our steps back to the entry turnstiles, back to the well-lit, poorly cleaned bathroom so that I could retrieve a tiny silicone-hydrogel bowl, spit on it, return it to its orbit & be visually functioning again. Did I mention my daughter was six? Did I mention that she held my hand & ignored me when I said, "are you sure we shouldn't go left?" I promise you this is true. In the taxonomy of learning I live at the bottom of the pyramid. Bound to my memories like Rumpelstiltskin to his straw. There's gold inside my hippocampus I'm sure of it. JD says this is just the beginning. The second level is understanding. As in—do you understand all the ways a person can die? As in—do you understand that every religion believes in the survival of the soul? As in—do you understand that there are zero degrees of separation between a Buddhist & a Baptist? Now construct a multiple-choice question. Provide diagrams & illustrations & flow charts. The way that every moment of my life flows like honey into the sticky current. The way that every funeral I've been to flows like a river of blackbirds. The way that my daughter & I returned to Hurricane Harbor & stood underneath the artificial waterfall like freshly baptized converts. If understanding is evolution, then I must understand that if I were a murderer, I'd use poison. Something slow acting like ricin. Or beautiful & toxic like oleander. Or painful & cruel like arsenic. Pay attention: this will be on the final exam.

If I were a murderer, I'd make a wrong turn when leaving the scene of the crime & end up in an empty field, low-flying airplanes lighting my way. If this is a hypothetical scenario. If the mirror behind the airport bar is a portal to my other lives. If I stayed home that night & refused the reaper's persistent knock. If memory is a nest full of sleepy wasps poisoned by smoke. Then what? If I were a good person, I'd never put out traps for spiders & mice. But I do. If I were a good person, I would have no fear of my judgment day. But I do. I tell JD I've reached my limit. I'll never advance to the third level. Instead I live with one simple truth. The answer to every single question is all of the above.

The First Day (1987) (redux)

I WAS NOT thinking about you in the elevator in New Orleans. One month away from the phone booth on a dirt road in Illinois. Corn fields. Your mother remembering my name. She told me you were married. Like a siren. Or the truth. In the elevator in New Orleans I was kissing someone else. Streetlight puddles bounced from the floor. 35 years later I don't remember his name. Your mother gave me your number. On the back of my hand was his tongue. On the back of my hand was a shortcut. If only you would answer. In the elevator. In the hall. On a postcard to my mother. I said wish you were here. I said we are having fun. The elevator door opened. I stared at the number 4.

Monday

I KNOW I have no right to complain. I promise I do. I know that every second of my suffering is mostly self-inflicted. My audacity is slimy. My suffering a tiny pea beneath 42 mattresses. I know I have no right to ask. But I don't want to do this anymore. Don't panic. I don't mean life. I mean my obsession with death. I cannot tell you what day it is. Or how many hours since I last spoke to you. It's a muddle of cherries at the bottom of the whiskey glass. Some days the world is a blue marble in my pocket. The world is a brisk sun storm. The world is a jungle of honeysuckle. Those are the good days. The world is a backyard parade. Sequins and glitter in the baby swimming pool. I know those days should be enough. I have no right to ask. But still I do. I ask you to remember me with something like regret. I remember that you changed cars like some people change shoes or lovers or time zones. Midnight blue: fire engine red: hospital black: harvest moon maroon. All smelled of cigarettes & Red Bull. Or cigarettes & green soap. Or cigarettes & sex because we could not wait for the bed on the other side of the door. The last time we spoke was in your newest car. I entered like someone enters a house where they used to live. Shag carpet & neon orange wallpaper replaced in favor of something more elegant & sterile: nothing to do with desire. You smoked the whole time. The whole time your cell phone was vibrating. At 2:15 a.m. on a Monday. I still wonder what you told her. I still wonder if anyone will tell you when I die. Will they know what you know: that I want to be buried in your flannel shirt: the one we laid out between two redbud trees on a cold April morning. My oldest blue jeans. Favorite boots. I wonder if you wrote our secrets on the back of your gas station receipt. Burned it with the last match from that hotel bar. I wonder if you will charge my cell phone. Tuck it in the torn pocket of that love-worn shirt. Oh please forget what I said when our hearts were stripped to sinew & blood. When another good child left this wicked life far ahead of us. In the rearview mirror you asked if I still love you. Call me. Ask me again. I'll answer from far below the field of yellow daisies. You'll know it's me because you won't believe a word.

The First Day (1981)

THE SOFA WAS brown: on this we can agree. I do not agree with your roses. Your guitar was blue. As blue as every lightning-ed sky I was waiting to see. Your guitar was blue: on this we can agree. I agree that your lips were not blue. Roundabout. Intersection. Waterfall. On this we do not agree. Me as a sleeping possum. You as the chord that wakes me from my dream. I could tell you that I remember every word you said. *Carnival. Backgammon*. You are not in the bedroom. Not in the laundromat stealing quarters for one more phone call. We were there. I know what you were wearing. Cut-off jean shorts. Red bowling shirt. Black Converse hi-tops. Your hair too long for our mothers. Have you figured it out yet? That this is a love story. That this is me forgetting all your sins. That the sofa is long crushed & buried. Also the roses. That I stole your guitar as I was leaving.

Acknowledgments

Grateful acknowledgment is made to the editors of the following publications, where some of these poems first appeared:

Louisiana Literature: "Tuesday"
Lumiere Review: "Wednesday"
Switch: "The First Day (2010)," "The First Day (2013)"

Beth Gordon is a poet, mother, and grandmother currently living in Asheville, North Carolina. She is the author of several chapbooks including *The Water Cycle* (Variant Literature), *How to Keep Things Alive* (Split Rock Press), and *Crone* (Louisiana Literature). Beth is managing editor of *Feral: A Journal of Poetry and Art*, assistant editor of Animal Heart Press, and grandma of Femme Salve Books. Twitter, Instagram, and BlueSky @ bethgordonpoet.

Belle Point Press is a literary small press
along the Arkansas-Oklahoma border.
Our mission is simple: Stick around and read.
Learn more at **bellepointpress.com**.

BELLE
POINT
PRESS